A Place for You

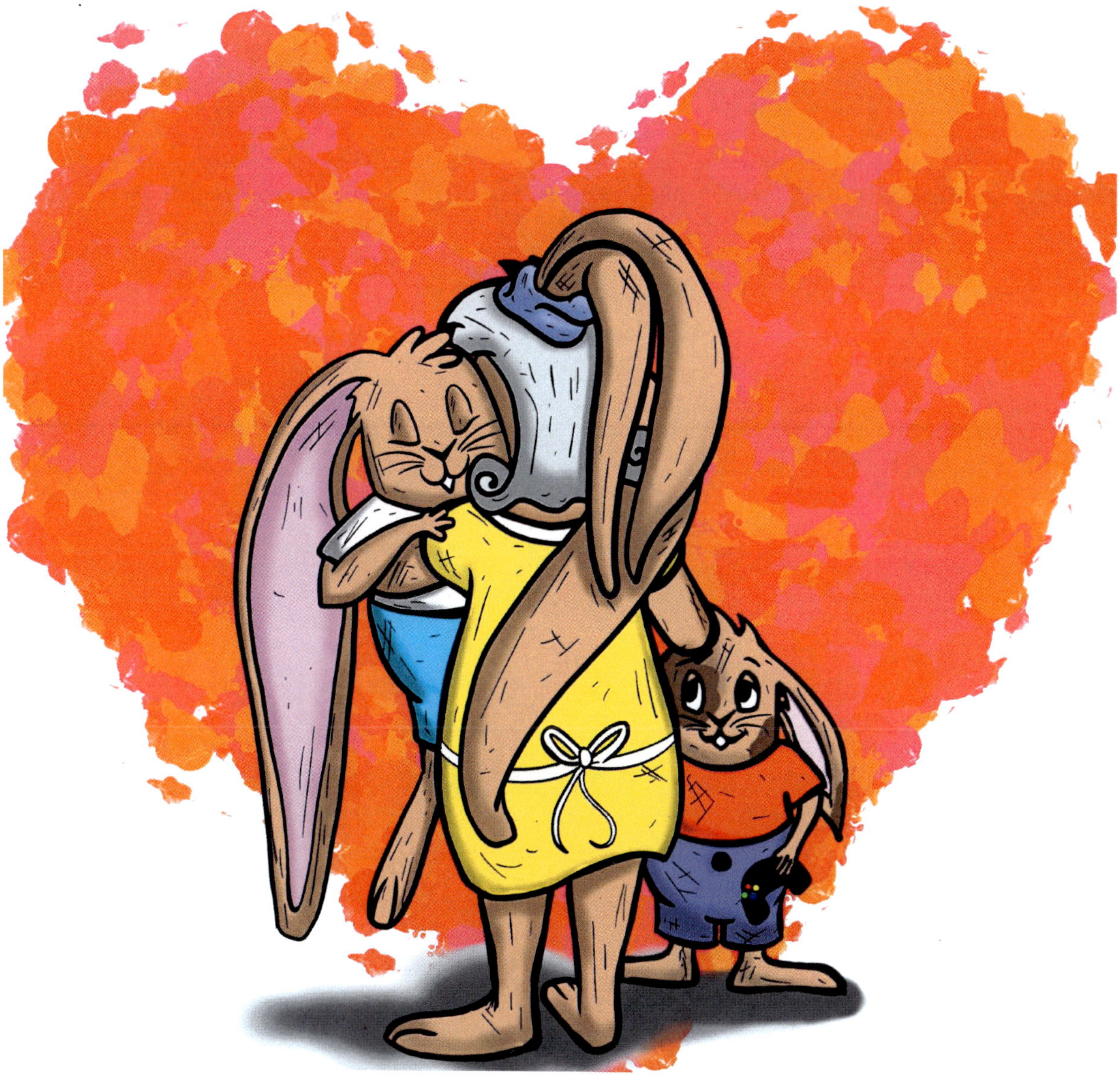

Thea Fielding-Lowe

Illustrations by Wesley Cruz

A Place for You

Illustrations by Wesley Cruz

ISBN: 978-1-7350328-9-4

Printed in the United States of America

Thea Fielding-Lowe is represented by T. Fielding Lowe Company, LLC.

T. Fielding Lowe Company, LLC.
T.Fieldinglowellc@gmail.com

This book belongs to

Make a list of everyone who is in your family,

How do you help your mom or dad?

"A Place for You" is dedicated to two bunnies, Jazariyah R. and Aiden G. Thank you for being my inspiration!

To the rest of the little bunnies in the world, you are all special and talented children. We will always love you no matter how many mistakes you make or how many trophies you win. God bless you all!

Today is going to be a great day! Little bunny thought to himself as he opened his eyes. I am going to help mom with the chores. When we are done, I will get a special treat.

Little bunny jumped out of bed and put on his clothes. He was moving super fast that he tore a hole in his shirt.

"Little bunny, please be careful and slow down." Mom said as she passed by the bedroom door. "You tore a hole in your shirt, because you were moving so fast."

"Sorry mom!" yelled little bunny.

Little bunny hopped down the stairs to the kitchen to eat breakfast. As he was pouring the milk on his cereal, he accidentally dropped the bowl on the floor.

"Little bunny, please be careful." "Take your time pouring your milk, so you don't make a mess next time" said mom.

Little bunny took a deep breath and said "I'm sorry mom." Then he went to the closet to get a mop to clean the milk off the floor.

The rest of little bunny's day was awful. He accidentally dropped the soda on the floor. He picked it up, put it back in the refrigerator and did not tell mom that he had dropped the soda can.

Mom was thirsty from cleaning, so she went to the refrigerator to get a drink. She opened the can of soda. Oh no! The soda sprayed in her face.

Next, little bunny tried to help with the laundry. He did not realize that he left his red sock in the wash machine after taking out the clothes.

Mom poured a basket of white clothes in the wash machine. Now all the clothes are pink.

The sink was filled with dishes. Little bunny tried to be helpful and wash them. He dropped a plate on the floor. The plate broke into a million pieces. Little bunny whispered to himself "I need to leave this house."

Little bunny's brother took his game. Little bunny got super mad and said a bad word. Now he is in time out.

"I want to leave this house" little bunny said, as he sat on the bed.

Today was suppose to be a great day. It's not. I have been getting in trouble the whole day. Some of it was not even my fault.

He thought to himself, I just need to leave this house.

Little bunny jumped off his bed. He went to his closet and took out his book bag. He hopped downstairs to the kitchen. Mom was cooking dinner. Little bunny filled his book bag with cookies and juice.

"Where are you going little bunny?"
Little bunny told his mom, " I need to leave this house."
Mom asked, "why do you need to leave?"

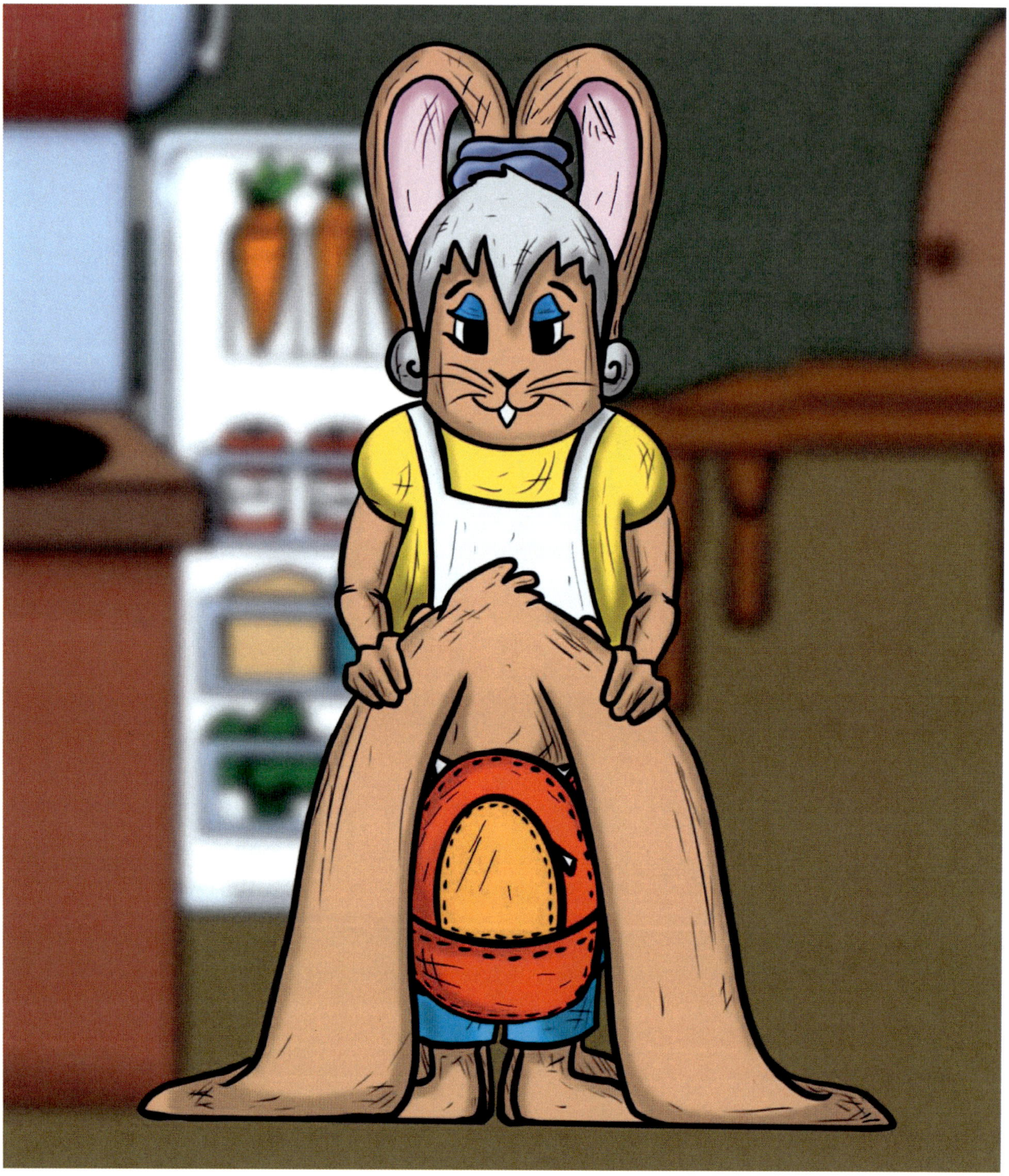

"I have made a lot mistakes today. I was suppose to be your helper."

Mom responded, "sometimes we make mistakes little bunny. That is okay."

" How can I make it better?" asked little bunny.

"You just need to say you are sorry. Remember it does not matter how many mistakes you make or how many trophies you win. Little bunny, there will always be a place for you in my heart and in this family. We all love you little bunny."

Color Little Bunny

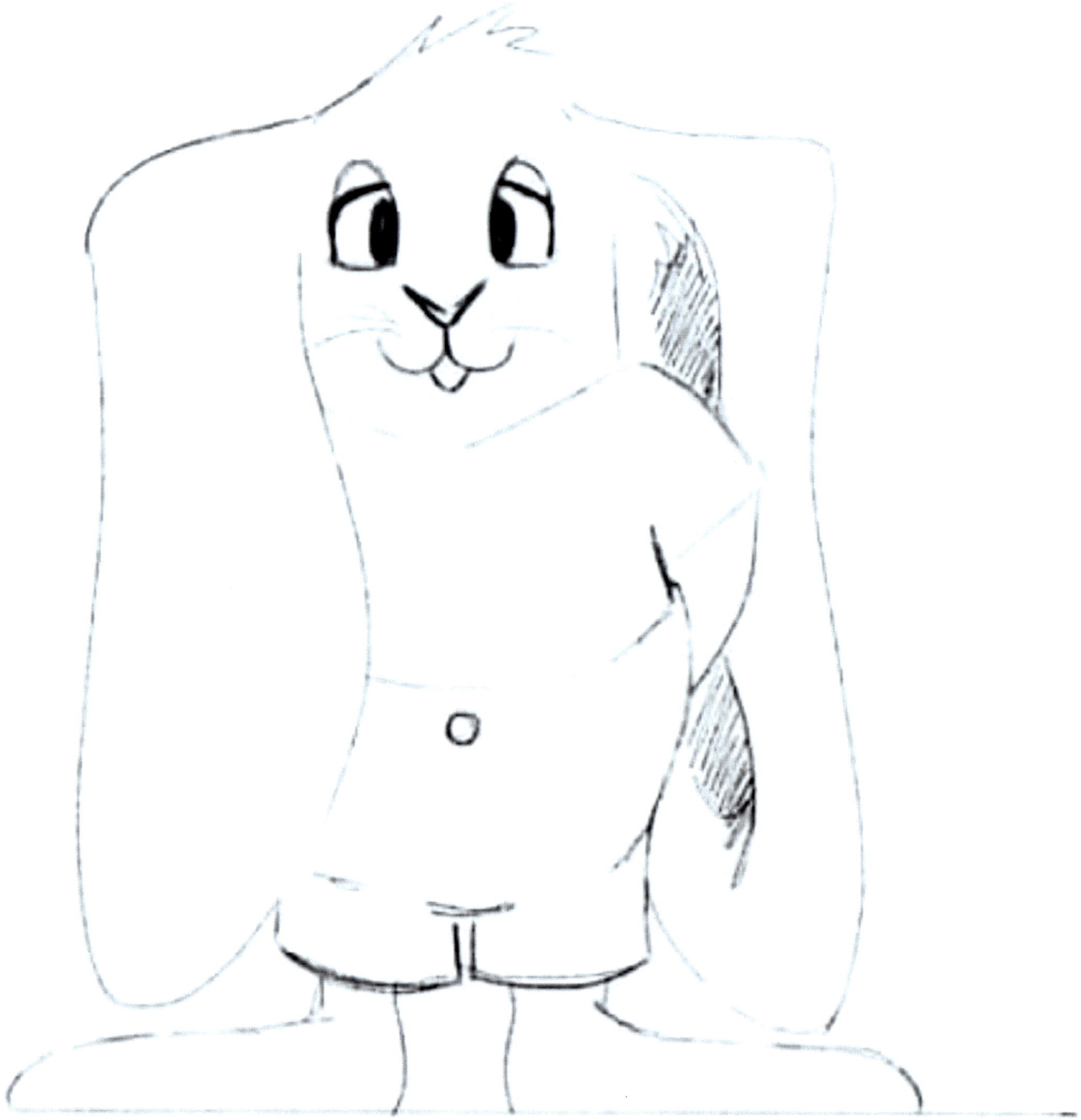

From the Author

Hi,

My name is Thea and I love to write books! I did not always like to read and write. When I was your age, I had trouble reading and had to get special help in school. At first, I would get frustrated, but after practicing, I realized that reading was easy. So don't give up!

I hope you liked reading "A Place for You". It was very important for me to let you know that you are loved. No matter if you make mistakes or you receive awards.

God Bless You!

Thea

Also Available on Amazon

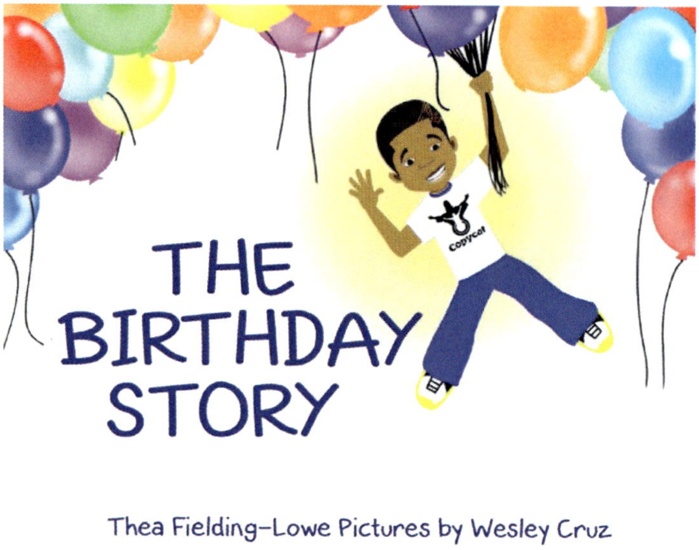

It's Jeffery's Birthday! Before God sends Jeffery to be with his mom, he blesses him with many gifts. His gifts include a new haircut, a shirt and pants from God's closet, the ability to play music, and most importantly a name. Jeffery is given everything he needs for the new world."The Birthday Story" is a great story to share with your children. It teaches them a basis of having a relationship with God and how God gives us everything we need before we are born.

"Hey Auntie, What Color is God?" Ysa asks her aunt, full of curiosity. Red, yellow, black or white -what will her aunt say? Purple.

This story is based on a conversation that the author had with her niece when she was four years old. Hey Auntie, What Color is God? is meant to be jump start a conversation about God and faith in addition teach the color wheel and learn vocabulary.

Made in the USA
Middletown, DE
07 June 2023

31966681R00015